FROM ONE SINGER TO ANOTHER

How to Sing Better, Be More Creative and
Have Some Fun While You're Doing It

Bruce Bennett

This book is dedicated to

Penny, who after all these years still
WHOOHOOS when I sing,
always inspires creativity in me,
and makes everything we do together
more fun.

And to all my students who trusted me
with their dreams and fears,
and taught me more than I could ever
hope to teach them.

———————————

Special thanks to

Penny Bennett, Darby Hollingsworth,
Marjorie Halbert, and Andy Catá for your
editing notes, gracious support, and
encouragement for this project.

Contents

Introduction

From One Singer To Another was written as a kind of recounting of the past fifty some odd years of singing myself and teaching others how to do it. I thought that if I helped Jean or Marvin or any one of hundreds of other students to sing better and be more creative, maybe I could help you, too.

Everybody sings at some time or other -- at church, school, around the holidays, and at birthdays. Some of us even get paid to sing. And though you may not want to make a career out of singing, there are

1

a few basic things you can do to sing better, to be more creative, and have some fun while you're doing it.

But, before I get too deep into things, I should probably tell you that this book ain't quite like the other books out there. 'Cause I have a little different way of thinking about singing and being creative. You might think of me as sort of a "mascot" for non-traditional thinking and unconventional teaching.

I have always enjoyed singing and I like telling stories, too. And like any good jazz musician and storyteller, I like making stuff up the best. So, that's how I teach, by telling old stories and made up new ones and then tying it all together to fit whatever situation might come along. That's how I help singers, like you, figure out for yourselves how to sing better and how to create what you want to create.

So, you might ask, "Where do I start?" Well, right where you are, of course, and with whatever you've got. Everything you need to sing and to be creative is right there inside of you. And, contrary to what some folks would have you believe, I don't think you need a degree in music or a PhD in anatomy to learn how to sing better. Although controversial and unpopular to traditional teachers of singing, I think you can teach yourself all you need to know. That's why I wrote this book, as a retelling of how I came to my own way of doing things, in hopes that it would help you find your own way of singing and being more creative. I hope it helps.

Chapter One
WHAT ELSE COULD I DO?

When I first started singing as a kid it was just for the pure fun of it. It was spontaneous and innocent, and I was surprisingly good at it for being so young. I can't say for sure why, but for as long as I can remember, singing just seemed natural to me. So much so that, sometimes in my shyness, it almost felt easier to sing than to talk.

I sang and walked up and down my neighborhood's streets, and sang when I rode my bicycle and jumped over ditches. I used to sing out loud as I wildly ran around the woods behind my house and

4

fearlessly climbed up to the very tops of the trees. I sang myself to sleep most nights and sometimes even woke up singing.

For me, singing was comforting somehow, like an old friend, always there, always growing and changing right along beside me as I grew and changed. Still, I never wished for or planned to become a singer. It just sort of happened, over time. One thing leading to another in the way things do when you're young.

Like for instance the first time I sang for my church's music director. I was twelve and for some unknown reason he had taken a liking to me or at least there was something about me that intrigued him. Either way, he asked me to sing for him, and after listening he invited me to join the adult choir. I joined at the next Wednesday night practice and not too long afterward I was singing all by myself doing special music at a Sunday evening service, which would be the first of many over the next few years.

And as the years came and went, lots of things happened, lots of things changed and just like every other teenager, somehow, I got through it all. But it was time then to move on and figure out what to do with the rest of my life. I knew going to college was expected of me, just like most of the kids that grew up around me. But I hated school.

The only thing I cared about was music. And the only thing I could do was sing. Luckily, during my senior year, I won the state high school solo festival and received a full-ride talent scholarship to study music. And so, without much more thought or hesitation, I headed off to college to major in music.

College was okay, but it was still school. And apart from finding the sweetest, prettiest girl I have ever known, I didn't get that much out of it. But, just so you know, I did get the girl and it has worked out beautifully, but that's another story all on its own.

So, despite my aversion to school and various other grown-up kinds of distractions, I somehow still managed to get a couple of fancy degrees from a couple of fancy schools. By then, I had done all the things I was supposed to do and now it was time to do what I wanted to do. And all I wanted to do was sing. So, that's exactly what I did.

I sang anything, anywhere, for anybody that would pay me. I sang at weddings and funerals. I competed in talent shows and even won a few. I sang in churches and bars, in restaurants, at conventions and trade shows from Texas to Maine, and carnivals and street fairs and colleges everywhere in between. I recorded and did session work in New York and Nashville, and actually got played on the radio, every once in a while, in a few of the smaller markets. One of the DJs said once, "the man definitely got skills," and aired an hour-long program of me singing. I did some TV work, mostly local stuff and even did some acting and directing in summer stock and regional theatres scattered around the country.

Sitting here now, looking back over all those years, I'm a bit sentimental about the things I've done and seen and heard and learned, and the lifetime of experiences and memories that have accumulated in my head. It all happened so fast. One minute I was this little creative kid just having fun pretending one thing or another and making stuff up out of my head, and then, I became the jazz musician, "smooth and sophisticated," a newspaper critic once called me. And now, well, I'm still singing, I think better than ever. But I teach now too, and I have to admit that it's all been pretty good -- better than I expected, that's for sure.

It's clear to me now that music chose me more than I chose music. There's probably a whole lot of other things out there that I could have done, if I had wanted to. But, I suppose, I just did what seemed natural and I did it long before I knew what it meant, or how hard it would be sometimes. Still, I love being a musician and singing. And I've been lucky to be able to make a living at it and even enjoy a little success over the years, although I never got famous or made a lot of money.

Looking back, I don't think I ever really wanted to be famous, although I probably could have. I was never willing to pay the cost for fame. And on top of that, the music business always seemed kind of sketchy to me. And I didn't want any part of that. I just wanted to sing and be in front of an audience. Now that's what I'm talking about -- frickin' amazing -- but it's the getting there that's a pain in the ass. They don't call it music "business" for nothing.

I learned all about the business part in New York City. It was different back then, before American Idol and the toppled record labels, and the creation of YouTube and iTunes. But even so, I learned what I had to do and what I didn't want to do. And sadly, the business of music has little to do with talent or creating music and everything to do with fads and quick money makers. But all I cared about was singing and being creative and getting to know myself, my likes and dislikes, my wants and needs.

Getting to know yourself is the key to learning to decide for yourself what to do and what not to do, and to find creative inspiration in your own thoughts and your own imagination. It can make a big difference in learning to sing better, since, **you are the instrument and the player**. To be creative and do creative things in your own way and your own time. And then, opening your mouth and singing out loud and not thinking too much about anything else.

There's something liberating about getting to know yourself and being in control of deciding what is best for you. It has taken me a whole lifetime to figure out all the things I can't do. And now I'm trying to figure out all the things I can do. But change comes slowly, sometimes. So, don't be too hard on yourself.

I'm still not quite sure how or when exactly the teaching side came into the musician part of me. It certainly wasn't something I expected to happen. 'Cause like I said before, I never saw myself as a teacher when I was young or at any other time, for that matter. And I certainly couldn't have imagined that I would be good at it and even grow to enjoy it. I still don't understand it, but it happened. And that's where I am now. I am a singer. That's what I am. But I'm a teacher, too, and truthfully, I can't imagine doing one without the other.

Chapter Two
WHAT IS IT YOU'RE MOST AFRAID WOULD HAPPEN—IF?

Over the years as I've thought about teaching and reflected on my own experiences singing, I've come to believe more and more in the idea that singing is more mental than physical, and more emotional than mental and physical combined. It's a kind of "mind-over-matter" type thing. Or more accurately, emotions over mind over body.

Let's look at, for instance, nervousness, it happens to everybody, on and off stage. It's a normal part of life. But where singers get into trouble is when they find themselves in situations where that kind of emotional thinking and uneasiness gets in the way of their singing. It's like the domino effect. Emotions affect thoughts. Thoughts affect breathing. Breathing affects your body. And for a singer that can be a precarious state to be in since their body is their instrument.

So, when you feel nervous, ask yourself why. Is it nervous excitement, as you smile at the audience and walk across the stage? Or are you worried about making a mistake and being embarrassed if things don't go as planned? Either way, "why" you do the things you do affects the way you think about things and "how" you go about doing them.

Consider this. Your body and mind are like this amazing mystery -- naturally perfect, uniquely spontaneous, and constantly changing. But as mysterious as it might be, figuring out how it all works, to the extent you are able, is an important part of figuring out the sound you want to make and making it sound good.

Singing is subtle to a degree, but with a whole lot of moving parts inside you all working together. So then, if everything is interconnected one can assume that any slight change will affect everything else. It's the law of nature. You change one thing and something happens to the other.

But you can't be afraid of change. It's happening everywhere, all around you. It's a part of life. So, you might as well learn to just go with it. Learn from it. Embrace the unexpected. Besides, that's when the good stuff happens anyway. That's when things get interesting. When your back is pushed against the wall and you have no choice but to figure out what you can really do.

I never knew for sure I could do what I did -- until I did it. I think that's true for most people, whatever they do in life. That's what I believe, anyway. That's why I spend a lot of my teaching days saying over and over again, "You never know what you can do until you try." You have to be willing to at least try something different. Unless you're too afraid of failing. That's when I pull out a line from one of my favorite Neil Simon plays, Chapter Two, that asks, "…what is it you're most afraid would happen--*if*…" Oh boy, you should see students' puzzled expressions then.

One of the very worst things about being afraid, it seems to me, is that it stops you from trying and doing new or different things. You get stuck. And sadly, you can't get unstuck because you don't really know what you're afraid of, and even when you do know, it's almost impossible to try to put it into words. I sort of get it though. Fear is a hard thing to understand and articulate, or even admit to, sometimes.

Kids are more adventurous and fearless, mostly because they haven't learned not to be. But us grown-ups get too caught up in the "what ifs" and "maybes," and too concerned with making a mistake, or worried about being embarrassed and uncomfortable, or even worse, being humiliated and looking like a fool. So, over the course of our lives we learn to be afraid. And then, our fears stop some of us from even trying.

I see that sort of thing all the time with students. Fear slowly creeps in, starting with the little things you can't do, but wish you could. And eventually, you end up not doing the things you know you should do.

You get a kind of tunnel vision and get so tangled up in being scared that you can't see or hear anything else around you. That's when you know you're stuck and that's when you have to figure out a way to get unstuck.

You have to face your fear. And ask yourself, "What is it you're most afraid would happen—if?" And, if you do, I almost certainly guarantee that the answer will push you in the right direction. Heading straight for getting unstuck. But you have to be patient. It takes a little time to get there, sometimes.

I think it's best to work from the inside-out, starting with the thoughts in your head and then, working your way down to the muscles in your body. Figure out in your own head the sound you want to make, then start trying to make it happen in the easiest way possible.

It's up to you to decide what works best for you. To trust yourself. To know when it feels right and when it feels wrong. And when you feel afraid and stuck, it's all up to you to feel and listen to everything you do and to find your own way to a freer, better sound. So, get out there and stop worrying about the bad things you don't want to happen and take a chance on some of the good things that might happen.

Chapter Three
YOU WANT ME TO DO WHAT?

I was always creative growing up. I mean, I don't remember one big moment when I suddenly got creative. It was just there, hanging around until I could decide what to do with it -- or not to do with it.

You see, southern boys, the ones I grew up around anyway, usually had a fishing pole in one hand and a hunting rifle in the other, and rotated from one sport to the next, depending on the time of the year. They didn't sing. At least not so as you could see or hear them. But even so, somewhere around six or seven, or maybe a little younger, I all of a sudden started to spontaneously burst into song. It was sort of like some kind of turrets. I couldn't help it. Which in some ways made it all the more awkward for me.

But, I was never the kind of kid that just went along with the crowd and did what was expected or what everyone else was doing. It didn't seem to matter if I was being made fun of and called names by other kids. Well, it did matter some, I suppose, but not enough to shut me up.

What can I say? I was a strong-willed and independent creative kid that liked doing my own thing and not worrying about trying to please anyone but me. I think, creativity does that to some people. It kind of frees you from worrying too much about what everybody else thinks and does. You learn not to care what others say and do, and to depend on yourself more than anyone else. To trust your own judgement and make your own decisions about what you should do and how you should do it. That's what being creative is all about. You look around at what everybody else sees and see something completely different.

Like when a little kid sees a rocking recliner chair and all of a sudden he's on a pirate ship in the middle of a raging sea. That's creative thinking! But, it's just an idea, he hasn't jumped up in it yet. Now, he has to decide. Is he going to play it safe or risk getting into trouble and have some fun? That's the hard part. You have to be the one to decide. And the older you get the harder it is to make that decision to let it all go and take the risk.

Clearly, some are able to do it more easily than others. Almost effortlessly. To let go and feel free to be creative and not worry too much about how it all turns out. To take chances and do something unexpected. But, I think it's in all of us to be creative. It's just a matter of finding your creativity and then, figuring out what to do with it. That can be a little tricky sometimes, but not impossible.

I've found the suggestion to go out and, "run nekkid in the woods," is a good place to start. To literally or figuratively find a quiet place and to strip away everything and then start from the beginning to get to know yourself -- inside and out. To experience yourself as who you are and genuinely question the ways you think and feel and believe.

Some young and inexperienced singers, some older ones too, don't always get it right away, and some don't get it at all. "You want me to take my clothes off and run around in the woods?" "No. It's imagery. What I want you to do is to create the experience in your imagination. To be open-minded and to imagine feeling free and totally unencumbered."

It helps to keep an open mind to learn, but even then, there's no right or wrong way to do it. For musicians, singers in particular, some need to see what's happening and then imitate it, whereas others just need to be told how to do something. And then, there are those of us who need to experience it ourselves before we can sing better and enjoy it more. But, no matter how you learn, at some point you have to be willing to trust what you've learned and just go for it.

You have to trust your own way of doing things because my way won't work for you and neither will anybody else's, no matter who they are. Every voice is different, just as every individual is different. And we all experience our own unique voice in different and very personal ways. It's about finding your own sound and figuring out on your own how to make it better.

It's about experience. I want you to go out and try stuff for yourself and don't get bothered by sometimes failing miserably. Just try over again and again, until you get it right. It's about persistence, not about being perfect.

Some folks really get caught up in the whole perfection thing because all their lives they've tried to be perfect in everything they do. But the truth is, the time and energy you save by being less than perfect can be used for better things. Like, learning how to work through problems on your own and take on challenges, or handle the unexpected things that most definitely will happen. 'Cause honestly, trying to be perfect is a waste of time and frustrating when it never happens. Not to mention, feeling defeated and stuck. That's never good.

It's not good for your mental health or your physical health, and it's definitely not good for your voice. Because whenever you feel stuck and frustrated and defeated, your body and mind automatically get tense. Your heart rate speeds up, your blood pressure rises, your breathing gets short and shallow, and then, the stress hormones kick in and the problems really begin.

Your muscles are in knots, you can't breathe well, your jaw and tongue get tight, your throat feels like it's closing up, you can't concentrate, and you can't sing. That's what tension does to you. It comes on slow and sneaky, sort of tiptoeing around and easing its way into your head and your body, and eventually, into your voice. And then, before you realize it, you get accustomed to the tension and that constant tightness in your throat starts to feel normal. It becomes a habit, and not a good one.

Singing should be effortless with no sound of strain or feeling of discomfort. Ideally you want it to be natural and relaxed, and spontaneous and free, and hopefully, enjoyable and fun. Well, maybe it won't be all those things all of the time, but it won't be any of those things if your voice feels tight and sounds forced, like a grunting sound you make lifting something heavy, or a kind of sharp harsh shriek. Those kinds of vocal sounds are signs of a problem that probably should be fixed and can be, with a little thought and some effort on your part.

It might be frustrating, at first. But, it shouldn't be too difficult to figure out what's interfering with your singing, since most problems, in some way or another, can be traced back to whatever emotion you're feeling at the time. Emotions affect everything -- what you think and what you feel, and sometimes even influence how you react. But, if you can figure out why you do the things you do, then, you'll be able to recognize the actions and behaviors before you actually act on them, and then change them by replacing the old habits with new ones.

Now how do I do that? Good question. Each phrase in singing should begin with a clean vocal sound, or clean "attack," which actually begins in your own head before you ever utter a single note. You have to start by figuring out the sound you want to make and then, find the easiest way to make it. The idea is to produce a relaxed open sound that flows freely out of you that sounds like your speaking voice, except more sustained and with the vowels drawn out a little more. You want to breathe naturally, open your mouth easily with every muscle relaxed and breathe out the gentlest tone in the most direct way possible. But, to make it a new habit, you have to be able to do it again and again.

In the beginning, there might be a little bit of a challenge between the new and the old way of singing. The old way, of course, will try to overtake the new way for a while. So, don't worry too much if you're not consistent right away. That's normal. Just keep correcting yourself. Go over it again and again, and keep going over it until it sticks. And then, after a while, the old **tight** way of singing will begin to feel unnatural to you and that's when you'll start to feel the old bad habits changing into good new ones.

Chapter Four
HOW DO YOU GET THERE?

My changeover from being, **just a singer**, with so-so habits, to becoming **a better singer**, with good habits, happened over time. Then, all of a sudden I got it. It all made sense. I figured out somehow or other, that I have to start from my emotions and decide what sound I want to make right then and hear it inside my own head before I sing a note. Then, sort of mentally pull together my ideas for how to go about doing it. After that, singing gets more physical and I have to put my ideas into practice and try to create the kind of sound I want.

I suppose, that's the trickiest part. Making everything that needs to happen all happen at the same time. At first, it seems like an awful lot that has to happen almost automatically really fast without thinking about it. But it's not that hard. It just takes a little time and practice. And, maybe, a little curiosity to figure out how to make all the moving parts work together. That's my favorite part, trying a little of this and a little of that to see what works and what doesn't.

I've always been curious, more so, even when I was a kid. I remember one time digging holes all around the yard with a spoon and imagining somehow I could dig one deep enough that I could make it all the way to China. Funny thing is, I didn't even know then what or where China was. It was just something I heard somewhere, and well, I was curious about it. I probably dug for hours and only stopped because the streetlights came on and I knew it was time to go in. I guess I don't have to tell you that I never made it to China, but it wasn't from a lack of trying, that's for sure.

The best I can say for myself in that disappointing failure is that at least I tried and that's the point. And I did learn that China was further away than I originally thought. You can't be afraid to try new things. Even if you fail, sometimes. How else will you ever learn anything or get better at something? You can't know why things happen the way they do or if something is going to work or not, until you "dig around," and try things out for yourself. And even if you don't find what you're looking for right then, at least you know more than you knew before.

Finding my own way is and always has been important to me, whether I'm singing or cooking or picking out a shirt. I don't care how I'm supposed to do things. And I most definitely don't care about the **Rules** handed down from on high by some authority deciding for everybody else what's good or bad, or best. I'd rather figure things out on my own and know for myself when it's right or wrong and whether it's good or not. That doesn't make me arrogant or a know-it-all. It makes me fortunate to trust my own gut feelings more than anything or anybody else. That makes me confident. Confident to be creative and to experiment with my own ideas without worrying about rules or how somebody else might do it.

I think rules undermine confidence a lot of the time. They chip away at it by answering the questions and solving the problems and making the decisions for you. Rules are just barriers intended to manipulate how you behave and react, as well as the things you say and think and feel. And when they're said strong enough and repeated often enough, you start to believe the rules and stop trusting your own thoughts and feelings. That's why I hate them. Because at that point, the rules are controlling your thinking.

Now, I'm not saying the world doesn't need some rules. For instance, the big "Thou shalt not" ones, like don't kill people and don't steal other people's stuff. Those rules make sense and we should certainly abide by them. Although, it's still sort of surprising to me that we have to be **commanded** to do what should come naturally. But even still, nowadays there are too many rules. I can't keep up with all of them. The old rules are always changing, new ones are constantly being added, and there are exceptions to all of them. There are even things that sound like rules that aren't rules at all, but rather some Joe Schmo's idea of how things ought to be. Rules are everywhere.

Even singing has rules. Although there's not a lot of agreement about what exactly the rules are. The rules mostly seem to me to be a lot of intellectualized jargon that's used to make singers feel like they must do something uncommon or exceptional and strictly controlled every time they sing. But in truth, the opposite is what actually happens. Singing is natural and spontaneous, and changes as we change. A singer's way of singing has to be personal and individual to their own unique instrument. No two voices are the same, just as no two people are the same.

So, look inside yourself and come up with your own way of singing that's totally new and different than anything anyone else has ever done or could do. Sure, there will be similarities to the ways others go about singing and meeting points with some of the basic ideas of singing, but no one else but you can know what feels right and what feels wrong, and what works best for you. I think, **whatever works is**

good and it doesn't really matter how you get there, as long as you get there.

I'm there. I've been there for a while now. Over time I found what worked for me – and what didn't. Then I started helping other singers learn more about how to do their own thing. And happily, most of them got there, too. They learned to trust themselves more and got to know themselves better. They sing better now than they have ever sung before. They create whatever they want to create and have fun doing it. And that's how I know you can get there. It might take ten minutes or it might take ten years, but either way, I promise it'll happen. You will change and grow for the better. It's just a matter of what you are willing to do to get there.

Chapter Five
ARE YOU READY?

Once you are able to do what you set out to do, it often doesn't end there. Things change. And just because you're there, doesn't mean that you've arrived. Learning to sing isn't about a one-time outcome or the end result. It's an ongoing process that changes again and again over   time.

And just when you think you've got it all figured out, something else changes. Your intellect grows. Your emotions mellow. Your body ages. Techniques that once worked for you become less effective. Even after years of successful singing you might still need to do some tweaking here and there. I certainly have, and still do.

That's one of the things I love most about singing. Everyday things are all together different, and yet familiar and identifiable. Every time I open my mouth to sing it seems there's always something new to figure out. Maybe, an unexpected sound that comes out of my mouth, or a new perspective to a song's words or melody. Those wonderfully curious things that I come upon that push me beyond where I am now. The constant push toward newness and change is what makes singing so fun for me, because that's who I am, although I didn't always know that about myself.

Although it might be a little scary sometimes -- change is good, I think. It's also necessary, which is what makes it oh-so-very good. It's about growing up and growing old. Change is about personal breakthroughs and new ways of doing things. It's about possibilities, thinking differently and whatever ingenious idea you might come up with. Change is about the way things can be rather than the way they are.

Stay curious and open to change. Look for opportunities to question. Trust your own thoughts and feelings more than anybody else's. Be willing to take risks and able to make choices, and then make the best of whatever choices you've made. And know that before you do things right you will probably do things wrong, and that's okay.

For me, change is about being ready for the challenge, whatever comes my way and having fun while I'm at it. Looking back, that's the only thing that I feel I didn't do that I wish I had done. To enjoy it all more. I think it might have had something to do with my creative life becoming my work and I forgot for a time how to have fun and enjoy it. It's important not to take things too seriously and to enjoy what you do while you are actually doing it. Otherwise, what's the point? That's a lesson I still hold with me today and have tried to pass on to other singers, too.

Change is natural. And it doesn't really do any good to worry too much about it, 'cause it happens whether you want it to or not. Everything changes at some point or other. Everything about you and around you will change. And funny enough, most times it happens when you least expect it. So, the thing is, expect the unexpected, and as crazy as it might sound, be ready for it when it happens.

Chapter Six
WHO ARE YOU?

Singing is natural and should be fun too, without feeling like work. That goes even for those of us lucky enough to be able to make a living doing it. What I'm saying is, it should be a good experience, not the stressful one some make it. It should be fun and enjoyable for everyone -- the singer, the other players, and the ones out there listening.

As children, we know this instinctively. Kids know it's all about playing and having fun. At first, singing is about childish words and silly tunes and making stuff up. But later, it's a kind of adventure of discovery, like when they hear their own voice for the first time.

I remember back when I was a kid, I used to tape myself singing all the time on my portable reel-to-reel recorder. It had its own handheld microphone that I sang into and then, I'd listen over and over again to my voice, playing back at me through the tiny little speakers.

But, like I said, **everything changes**. We get older and get caught up in our grown-up life and without even noticing, we forget how to enjoy ourselves and have fun. We forget the satisfaction and enjoyment that comes from doing creative things, like painting and dancing and singing. We forget how to play. We start worrying too much about what everybody else might say or do. Or that maybe things won't turn out like we want them to. And then, slowly over time, we stop doing things that we were good at and that we used to enjoy.

I'm reminded of a young woman who came to me for help many years ago. She was mid-30s at the time, and mostly sang in the choir at her church and for her own enjoyment, but she was having a hard time doing either one.   She described a "choking feeling," and said, "It feels like I have something stuck there," motioning to her neck. I asked her to sing for me and within the first few notes I could hear the tightness in her voice and see the tension in her neck. I stopped her right away as soon as her voice cracked and asked, half-jokingly and half seriously, "Why are you choking yourself to death?"

Her eyes sort of narrowed a bit and she got this blank look on her face that told me I probably needed to explain myself. "Certain kinds of emotions you carry around with you are going to affect your voice and change your natural equilibrium. Your throat hurts because you sing with a lot of tension in your neck. You are literally choking yourself.   The tension shows everywhere -- in the constricted muscles in your face and neck, in your clinched jaw, and in the tightness all around your mouth and tongue. It shows itself in the way you hold your body and it affects your breathing." I asked, "What's going on with you when you're doing this?" The answer didn't come right away.

It didn't come the next week or the week after that either. As a matter of fact, several weeks went by before the answer came. And it seemed to come to her as unexpectedly as the question had. She recalled a day when she was a little girl singing in the backseat of the family car and her dad angrily yelling at her to stop singing. She remembered feeling embarrassed and ashamed, and then sort of shrinking into silence. "Well, there's the problem," I said. "You are unconsciously choking off the sound to stop yourself from singing. You're protecting yourself from having hurt feelings again."

Almost immediately, her thinking changed and she understood why she had always felt shy and nervous about singing in public. It was funny, she seemed somehow relieved that it was all in her head, not her throat. And like that, everything changed. She found her confidence again and her voice came back, too.

Now, maybe you can see how your emotions live in your head and affect everything you think and do. It's being in your head that makes it real, and sometimes, gets in the way of you doing the things you want to do.

We all see and feel things differently. I see the world and everything in it through my own filter of crazy emotions. And I react to things based on my own skewed beliefs, irreverent opinions, and unique collection of life experiences and memories. It's all of these differences that make us who we are and shapes the way we react to, and think about, whatever happens to us.

Who you are answers everything. Well, maybe not everything but, it answers a lot of things. Like, why you do the things you do and how you go about doing them. My point is this, knowing and accepting who you are is a big part of growing and learning and understanding. And once you know yourself better and understand why you do what you do, you can then figure out how to sing better and be more creative.

Now isn't that what we should be concerned about most? Thinking different. Looking different. Singing different. And, well, just being different. I don't particularly want to think or look or do anything like anybody else. I never have. It seems unnatural to me to do or say the same thing as somebody else has already done and said.

I feel the same way about mimicking other singers too. I know a lot of people do it for a lot of different reasons, but it seems mainly to be an issue of not knowing who you are or who you want to be. The truth is, when you try to sound like another singer, it says to me that you don't trust your own natural talent and creative imagination so much so, that you're willing to give up the unique qualities of your own individual voice.

I think that's a mistake. Because to sound like someone else, you have to affectedly change the natural qualities of your own voice by manipulating and tightening your instrument in unnatural and maybe even harmful ways. And that's how singers who try too hard to sound like other singers wind up with a lot of vocal problems and consequently, struggle to find their own natural way of singing.

But aside from the potentially unintended vocal problems connected to mimicking, there is the seemingly obvious practical matter of why anybody would want to listen to an imitation when with radio, TV and the internet, they can just as easily hear and enjoy the original. And even though some imitators can technically duplicate, to some degree, another singer's sound, everyone knows that it is never as good as "the real thing," -- 'cause nobody can do you better than you can do yourself.

As a singer, I always felt like I'd rather be disliked for doing me, than liked for pretending to do somebody else. So, I never tried to sound like anybody else but me. But, besides that, I like the voice I was born with. It suits me. And I bet, if you think about your own voice, it probably suits you, too. So, why not start with what you have and work from there.

I tell my students all the time that, "Your natural voice and creativity are gifts, but what you do with them depends on your attitude and the way you think and see things." The gifts come with the house, so to speak. They're a part of you. But it's who you are that determines what you do with them. It's your choice whether you grow and learn. You decide whether or not you are going to use what you were born with.

So, get to know your own voice. Listen to it. Trust your instincts about what you do or don't do, and be confident and believe in the voice you have, not the one you wish you had. And learn how to relax and breathe. If you do this, I promise you that you will sing better and easier, and you'll enjoy it more.

Chapter Seven
ARE YOU BREATHING?

Breathing is a habit in the way habits are repeated regularly and without much conscious thought or effort. It's naturally inconspicuous and one of those involuntary habits, or actions, that mostly go unnoticed. That is unless you stop doing it altogether. But aside from something unfortunate like that, you don't really think about it. Can you imagine if you had to think about every breath you took throughout the day and night? You'd scarcely have little attention left for anything else. Luckily for us, some habits, like breathing mostly take care of themselves.

Breathing is one thing most of us feel we already know a little something about, a sort of street-smart knowledge we've gained just from experience. It's funny that most people don't realize there's a wrong way to breathe or that there's even such a thing as bad breathing.

Good breathing is naturally a part of being relaxed, like the way our minds and bodies relax when we sleep. I always tell students that the best teacher for good natural breathing is a sleeping baby. You can see their stomach naturally pooch out as the air smoothly moves into their lungs and then out, with the movements of the diaphragm, slowly, deeply and rhythmically, freely filling the lungs with air and rejuvenating their little body and mind.

But oh, how things change as we get older and we come to realize that life can really suck sometimes. And in those sucky times, if we let them, our emotions and our heads can get the better of us. And what's the first thing that happens? You get short of breath and your heart speeds up.

It hasn't happened in a long time, but I've been there myself. Like this one time, a long time ago, I was involved in a car accident on the way to a performance of *Amahl and the Night Visitors*. I was playing King Melchior.

I stopped to pick up my costume and just as I was making a left turn into the parking space, another car plowed into the side of my car while trying to pass from behind. My car was damaged but drivable, so after dealing with the other driver and the police, I headed on to the theatre.

At first, I seemed okay, shaken a bit naturally, but still okay. The show went on and so did I, and we both were clicking right along fantastically when all of a sudden it was time for my big aria, "Oh Woman You Can Keep That Gold" and, silence. Nothing! I went up on my lines. I was completely blank. I couldn't remember the first words of the aria. I started sweating. I couldn't breathe. I couldn't think. And what was actually only a second or two seemed like an hour. Then, from what seemed from out of nowhere the actress playing Amahl's mother knelt down beside me and softly sang the first line into my ear -- just in time for my entrance.

Right away, I refocused my thoughts and got my emotions in check. I had prepared as well as I could and now I had to trust myself. I had to trust my experience and let it guide me. I eyed my mark at center stage, and calmly and majestically moved into the spotlight. I instinctively took a deep slow breath to relax my body. And then, without thinking, I felt my mouth open and heard my voice coming out of it. It wasn't perfect, I'm sure, but I was singing.

The truth of the matter is that every person, every day, has to face difficult situations, and do things and make decisions about things they're not prepared for or expecting. Of course, with any luck, it doesn't happen in front of an audience -- but still stuff happens. Life is funny that way. It's full of surprises.

But, in those unpredictable times paying a little more attention to the way you breathe can be helpful. To be more aware of changes and shifts in a normal and natural way of breathing to what I call, "survival breathing" that sort of fluctuates between not breathing at all and short shallow breaths. If you find that you are regularly breathing badly, partially holding your breath or breathing shallow and you want to relearn to breathe naturally, it's probably a good time to learn a little bit about how it all works.

The diaphragm is the breathing muscle and muscles have memory. And when situations which bring out emotions, like anxiety and worry, reoccur over and over in your life, they often alter your natural way of breathing and reinforce the muscles' memory. It's subtle at first and you probably won't even notice a difference. You inhale, you exhale. You talk, you sing. Everything is working fine. It's amazing. But just because it all seems to take care of itself without you even being aware of it, it doesn't mean your breath is free flowing and necessarily giving your body what it needs to function well and feel well.

You might need to figure out if you are a good breather or not. It's not necessary to make a big deal out of it or over-complicate things by over-thinking it. But to just give your breathing a little focused attention and see if you happen to notice any trouble spots, and then move on and let whatever changes that might need to happen, develop in an organic, natural way.

Here's an easy way to find out if you're a good breather or a bad breather. Lie down on the floor and place one hand just below your ribcage on your abdomen, and then, slowly draw in one full deep breath through your nose. Then once your lungs are full and you begin to exhale through your mouth you should be able to feel the pooch as your abdomen rises and falls back in to place. That's natural good breathing. Remember that you have control over how you breathe and how you breathe affects everything -- how you think, how you feel, and for those of you who sing and want to sing well, breath affects that too.

Now, I could go on and on about the concepts of breathing and about all the conflicting opinions and contradictory arguments. But I will stop here, and simply say, "just breathe," and let's move on.

Chapter Eight
ARE YOU LISTENING?

I've already talked about good breathing, its normal conditions and the importance of being relaxed and at ease. I've also mentioned hearing the notes in your head before you sing them, but I didn't talk about how important it is to pay attention to what you hear.

As musicians, especially singers, we sometimes forget the importance of our ears as a focus of our attention; and so, we end up spending all our time focusing on making sounds, not listening. But, listening is as much a part of being a good musician as playing and singing. We listen to learn and create, to practice and perform, to critique and teach, and to simply hear and appreciate our own or someone else's performances.

I think most musicians, whether we are working or not, listen in an **active**, or concentrated way, always paying close attention to the sounds being made all around us. We hear things differently from everyone else and we also hear different things. Sound is about perception and recognition and connecting what we hear with what we want them to hear. Them being the audience, the ones who mostly listen in a **passive**, almost lackadaisical way with little or no concern for what they hear. The ones that listen to music, but do something else at the same time, like drive or work on homework or cook and clean. For them, music is background and they are mostly unaware of the creative experience that's happening around them.

Music is different for everybody for the simple reason that everybody is different. And why we listen affects the way we listen. For instance, singers do a lot of "inner hearing." That is, self-listening, or listening to how they sound while singing.

I call it, "listening with your musical ear," which is your own inner hearing and imagination working together to create in your mind the sound you want to make, and then, helping your voice and body to actually create the sound out loud. Because singers are the instrument and the player, that makes us a little bit different from other musicians.

It can take some practice to get the hang of at first, but once you've been doing it for a while, it gets easier. You find your equilibrium and get better at fine-tuning your voice by what you hear and by how it feels. It's like dancers who dance in front of mirrors in the studio to study their movements and compare what they see in the mirror with how it feels in their bodies. Then, when they're on stage, they know without looking what their body is doing and what the audience is seeing. That's called muscle memory, or some people say "procedural memory," and it works pretty much the same for everybody. It's when you practice or do something over and over again until your muscles start to remember it. Eventually you can do it automatically without thinking. We all use muscle memory whenever we do things like go up and down stairs, ride a bicycle, or catch and throw a football.

For those of us who play and sing music, muscle memory, along with a good musical ear, is how we are able to go back and consistently create a good, or better, sound without thinking about it. It becomes our technique, which means, "the way you go about doing something." But also, being able to do it, over and over again, without thinking about it. It's figuring out why things happen and learning how things work.

Why things happen is almost always on you -- your natural talent and ability, your habits, who you are and how you think, and the choices you make. Simply put, it's why you do the things you do the way you do them. And on the flip side of that, how things work has nothing to do with you because most of the things you do and don't do are automatic. Your mind and body naturally work the way they are intended to work, that is, unless you interfere with them.

Now, I'm not saying that singers don't need to know a little about the technical stuff for themselves. But, I am saying, "concentrating too much on technique, just gets in the way of everything." You get caught up in a whole lot of thinking and not a lot of doing. And I believe some things you learn better by doing. So, if you really want to sing, then start singing. And if you don't like what you hear, inside your head or out, try doing something different.

I told you already about recording myself and listening back. Well, when I was a kid, I used to listen and make up all kinds of weird sounds and improvise melodies. I'd sing them over and over, probably, a hundred times or more before I could get my voice to feel and sound the way I wanted. That's how I figured out what worked and what didn't. I listened and I experimented.

Chapter Nine
WHAT ARE YOU DOING?

I've been talking a lot about how I did things and how I made up my own mind about things, instead of having it made up for me. Sometimes, I made funny faces, sticking my tongue out at the mirror, and made all kinds of weird noises. I tried any and every peculiar thing that came to my mind. I looked and listened carefully and then played around with the things that bothered me. Every time I tried something, I paid close attention to what I was doing when things would get better. Then, I'd just do more of that, and less of everything else. And that's how I found my own special knack for singing.

By the time, I had reached my late twenties, I had this whole singing thing figured out. I had found my balance and my own way of doing things. But, how I did things doesn't necessarily make my way better or not as good as others. It just makes it different. And not different just for the sake of being different, but because it works.

Doing something different is always an experiment that, of course, comes with no guarantees of how things will turn out. And, in my humble opinion, "different is always better, even when it's not." But you can't be scared. You gotta go for it. Try something you wouldn't ordinarily try, and don't worry about getting things wrong a time or two before you get them right. Just keep playing and experimenting until you get the sound you want. And that's how you'll find your own technique.

Technique is a practical thing for singers who are concerned with practical stuff like good breathing, opening your mouth correctly, and focusing on vowel sounds as you sing. It shouldn't be about whether you can, "la-la-la" and "do-re-mi," or make silly buzzing sounds with your lips, or pant like a dog. None of that particularly means you are going to sing better. It just means you vocalize well and can repeat a lot of boring, inane exercises.

Although not a new or even original idea I don't routinely use a lot of repetitive exercises in my teaching. I don't see the point in externalizing or separating the problem from the music. After all, the problems exist in the music and should be dealt with as they come up. I also think exercises make singers view themselves as the problem and limits the ways they can effectively fix whatever needs fixing. So, it should come as no surprise that I steer clear of the more traditional approaches to singing. Exercises just seem counterproductive to me. Besides, it's a pretty far jump from making isolated sounds to actually singing songs and creating music.

Technique develops over time, little by little, as you accumulate experience and grow as a musician. It becomes spontaneous and instinctive to react to circumstances or limitations as they happen. That's why I believe you learn to sing better by singing and that the right song will teach the voice. You learn by hearing and feeling, and sometimes even seeing. You learn to adapt and just make it up as you go along.

I've already talked enough about breathing and it seems ridiculous for me to say over again, "You have to open your mouth to sing." But I will anyway, because it's important to know that the amount of space that is created by the position of your mouth has everything to do with the sounds that are going to come out of your mouth. Space affects sound. That's basic acoustics. And it's hard to get a good sound with your jaws clamped shut, or tongue curled up and back, and your throat muscles constricted, or your mouth forced open incorrectly and too wide.

You create space inside your mouth by resting your tongue flat and forward, and keeping your throat open and relaxed. Your mouth should open naturally, easily dropping down and slightly back. You should be able to feel the open space in your mouth and throat. It's the **openness**, that allows the vowels to narrow or widen and lengthen and ring out more clearly. The more space, the better the sound.

Space also helps to shape the vowels, as well as, keeping them closely connected as you move from one to the other. And be sure to keep in mind that the move from one vowel to the next should be almost imperceptible, without any change or interruption of the tone no matter how many or what consonants come in between.

You sing vowels and gently, but quickly articulate consonants to communicate words. You should spend a little time focusing on vowels, like those found in the words, h[a]t, [e]gg, [i]tch, [o]dd and [u]gly. Sing a melody line from a song. Pay attention to how each vowel feels in your mouth and sounds in your own ear as you move from one vowel and one word to the next. You can even use a mirror to look at how subtle changes in your tongue and mouth position affects the sound of the vowels. It takes a lot of experimenting over-and-over again, trying new things until you get the sound you want. And when things aren't working the way they should, don't be afraid to change what doesn't work and add what's needed.

It's all common sense really. Listen to your gut. Hear your own voice do things you've never known it to do. Experiment with all kinds of sounds. Face the mirror and watch yourself. Hear new possibilities for yourself. Look inside your imagination and see what you can create.

You might have to go back and read the last few paragraphs again. But if you're okay with making silly faces and funny noises, you can figure it out. Just like I did, pay really close attention to what you are doing when things get better then, do more of that and less of everything else. That's how you'll find your own technique.

Chapter Ten
WHAT'S YOUR RUSH?

It took a whole lot of singing over-and-over again and fixing what needed fixing before I got the sound I wanted, and settled into my own way of singing. It wasn't too hard, really, but it was frustrating sometimes, that's for sure. I suppose it's always frustrating when you try to change a bad habit to a good one. But you can do it if you bring together the sound you hear in your own head with the one you want coming out of your mouth. It just might take a little time to find the right balance.

Unfortunately, these days we live fast lives in fast times with new ideas and newfangled technology moving at lightning speeds all around us all the time. Faster internet speed. The newest iPhone version. Instagram. And, out of all this craziness we've come to expect fast results and quick fixes and "Five Easy Steps..." to a flatter stomach or banking a million dollars. But, getting better at some things doesn't really happen like that. With some things, like singing, the right balance and understanding that eventually leads to getting better comes a little at a time.

I sort of think it happens in subtle unexpected ways. For instance, if you do not have the vocal range demanded by a particular song you want to sing, there are things you can do to move toward the range you want. You first begin with exploring the lowest to the highest pitches of your voice that you presently sing with ease and flexibility. Then, start extending the range of your voice note-by-note and blending smoothly the different range of tones in your voice into a continuous whole, or **one voice** that feels and sounds the same from top to bottom.

I told you early on that I used to sing riding my bicycle all around the neighborhood. I must have ridden up and down those streets a million times pretending that I was a policeman in hot pursuit, or a fireman on his way to a blazing fire; all the while imitating the sound of a siren, sliding my voice from low to high pitches and back down again. Although I didn't know it at the time, this is actually a pretty common way for a singer to smooth out the bumps and even out their voice from top to bottom. I suppose you could even call it an exercise. But it wasn't work to me at the time, it was play.

Like I said before, "It's really just common sense." You start out making silly noises and before you know it you've put together a whole string of notes without even thinking about it. You figure it out as you go, and if it doesn't feel right, you try something different. You try seeing and hearing and feeling things that you didn't or couldn't see and hear and feel before. You find your balance.

Balance is one of those mysterious laws of nature that's extremely personal and means something different for every singer. It can't be forced or rushed or manufactured. Balance is that delicate connection between the mental, the emotional, and the physical. And is usually better left to itself to settle into its own equilibrium naturally with as little interference as possible. You can't force balance. For singers who want to sing their best or just want to sing better, balance means connecting what you hear and how it feels when all the working parts are doing what they're supposed to be doing.

I found my balance while I was playing the role of Jesus, hanging there on the cross in a performance of *Jesus Christ Superstar*. It would seem that all my years of experimenting and making silly noises somehow unexpectedly came together in this wonderful moment on stage. I could feel the warmth of the spotlight on my face, my arms extended forming the shape of the cross as the sound of my own voice overpowered me. It was effortless to me, every word and every note free of any noticeable technique. My voice carried even the softest note clearly ringing through the theatre. Everything felt in sync. And for the first time, I found my balance and I knew without a doubt that every note that came out of my mouth would sound and feel that way from then on.

Not a whole lot has changed between then and now. Still, whatever naturally and most easily comes out of my mouth with the least amount of physical effort, that's what I do and usually without even thinking about it. I should probably take a second and point out here that it was merely a coincidence that I finally found what made singing better for me while I was playing the role of Jesus. I wouldn't want you to think there was anything divine or mystical that transformed the way I sang. It was just the right time and the right balance after a whole lot of experimenting and a bunch of time doing things over-and-over again that I finally found what worked for me and I stuck with it.

Chapter Eleven
WHO DO YOU TRUST?

There's already a whole lot of books out there that talk about singing. They all pretty much say the same thing in some way or other, and they usually take a whole bunch of pages to say it. But what most of them don't tell you is that **singing is more about what's going on in your head than what's going on in your throat.**

In most all of those other books, they make singing more about the mechanics and less about just plain old good singing. They rarely mention having any kind of fun. They mostly talk about the "art" or the "science" -- the nuts-and-bolts of singing. And, whether intentionally or not, they just sort of skim over the real truth that singing is mostly in your head.

It begins in your imagination. You get an idea about what you want to sing. You start to hear the notes in your own musical ear. You imagine the sound of your voice inside and outside of your head. And at the same time, your body starts to respond to all the creative things going on in there. You inhale. You exhale. You open your mouth and extraordinary things happen. Well, at least that's what you hope for.

But, the imagination can sometimes be a hard-to-tame monster, wildly emotional and impulsive. Take it from one who knows from first-hand experience. Singers can be a bit emotional, at times. And sometimes their emotions throw everything out of kilter and get in the way of their singing.

That's the hardest part about singing, I think. Learning how to coordinate the mental stuff with the physical, and all without interfering too much in the natural flow of things. I suppose if there is a secret to singing, or life in general, it is learning how to get out of your own way. To not sabotage yourself by getting caught up in too many thoughts about too many things. Of course, early on I had no idea what that meant exactly.

Growing up, nobody ever tells us that it's just as risky to think too much as too little, or that if we just relax and trust our instincts we will eventually find our way to whatever we want to do. It took me a while to figure that out. However, the more I lived life and worked around other musicians, the clearer it became to me that we all can, and often do, get in our own way with all kinds of self-defeating behaviors.

Stuff like being afraid and not trusting your own instincts. Or getting stuck overthinking everything. Or holding on to old habits instead of taking up new and better ones. And by forgetting the most important thing of all, that even if things don't work out the way you hope they will, all you have to do is try something different. It's okay to try again. To imagine, to hear, and feel something different.

While all of the things I've been talking about go into being a good, or better, singer and being more creative, it all means nothing without confidence. You need to have confidence in who you are and what you do. It's something to build on, to learn and grow, no matter what you are trying to do. And besides, without confidence, how in the world do you expect others to be there for you? And what's music without somebody to be around to hear it?

I think, keeping a clear head and having a clear focus, and feeling free creatively and vocally, gives an enormous boost to your confidence and makes singing easy and relaxed, while feeling natural and sounding spontaneous. It just happens instinctively, automatically -- without thinking about it. I believe singing should always feel like that. Effortless.

Of course, it will take effort at first to figure out doing things your own way. To think differently makes you feel differently and do differently. But if you feel it's easier to do what everybody else does or what you've been told to do whether it feels right to you or not, well, you may be a little uncomfortable with the idea of stripping down and finding your own way.

It may be a little scary for some of you to step out on your own and to stop thinking the way that everyone else thinks. Though that wasn't the case for me. I suppose I was too stubborn or rebellious, and somehow had decided pretty early on that I was going to do things my own way on my own. And luckily, once I stepped outside of myself and began to question and find answers on my own, that's when all kinds of possibilities opened up for me. Possibilities I didn't even know existed inside me.

I suppose it was around this time I started to look at singing as an **inside job**, meaning that we can only sing as well as we can think. And that's why I believe so strongly that what goes on in your head is way more important to singing than what goes on in your throat. It's our brain that tells our voice what to do, but it is how we use our imagination that fills in what happens in between. That's where all the creative stuff happens, where you reshape old ideas or come up with completely new ones, and you think things you've never thought before.

But, you don't want to think and ponder too much. Eventually, you have to stop thinking and start "doing." That's what helps you get better. You have to figure out what you want and what problems you want to solve, and then get out of the way and trust your imagination to do its creative work. Even if you are not sure where it will lead.

You have to trust yourself. And if you don't already, maybe it's time to ask yourself, "why," you don't trust yourself? Maybe you tried a lot of things and they didn't work out, or you are afraid of what people will say if you fail. But, you have to learn to care more about what you think of yourself than what others think of you. And, if you want to sing better and be more creative, you have to figure out what you need to do to get past those feelings and change things. Somehow you have to learn to listen closely to your own instincts and be smart enough to hear them and brave enough to trust them. You have to let go of any fears and completely surrender to your imagination. And no matter what happens, use every experience to learn something you need to learn, not just about singing, but more importantly about yourself as someone who just so happens to sing.

Chapter Twelve
ARE YOU HAVING FUN YET?

I still experiment all the time, trying this and that to see what may happen with my voice and maybe create some interesting new sound. I've been doing it since I was a kid, pretending to play the piano while having all sorts of fun singing. I can't tell you how many hours and days I sat on my grandmother's ottoman running my tiny fingers along the edge of the sofa playing an imaginary keyboard and singing whatever came into my head.

It wasn't too long before I started taking real piano lessons with a lady from my church. It was all fun at first, the white keys and black keys, the sheet music full of all kinds of notes and rhythms, not to mention the wonderful sounds coming from every direction.   But then it got to be uninteresting after a while – even painful, sometimes. My enthusiasm really cooled down and I decided that singing seemed to be more my thing. So, I happily gave up the piano lessons.

I still played while I sang, probably more than ever because it was fun again. There were no more hours of repetitive practice or abusive lessons chipping away my confidence. I was free to be creative and to play and sing what I wanted, the way I wanted to play and sing it. There were no expectations, no rules, no pressure. It became about the music again and using my imagination the way it used to be before I started taking those damn lessons.

I sort of think it was around this time that I first decided that I didn't have to take lessons to be a musician. I don't remember for sure, but I probably thought, "I can figure this out for myself." And in the end, that's what I did. I became my own best teacher.

Not that I was a know-it-all or a prodigy, or anything like that. There was plenty I didn't know, but there was plenty I did know too -- common sense kind of stuff. Stuff I figured out by trusting and following my own gut instinct. You don't need a degree in science or music to figure these things out. Don't misunderstand. I think a lot about a lot, but in the end, I trust that inner voice more than anything else to tell me everything I need to know.

To me it was just plain old horse sense to know that my voice needed air to work properly. So, I figured out how my breathing worked and how the air affected the sound. And it seemed only logical that I had to open my mouth if I wanted anybody to hear the wonderful sounds I was making. I also figured out that any tension or obstruction, like tight throat muscles or when my tongue humped up, unnaturally changed the sound of my voice. It somehow, even back then, made sense to me.

Some years later at college, I was taught exactly what everybody else had been taught. And after all those years of schooling, I was well exercised and technically trained in an entirely different way of singing. It had become all about the "art of singing," -- the mechanics -- and nothing much about the feeling of singing, so I sort of lost myself for a while.

I understood what I was learning, but when it came down to it, I didn't like the conventional approach to singing. It always felt peculiar to me. I had my own ideas about singing and creating music. But in all honesty, their ideas weren't all that different from mine, really. It just felt that way to me. I think it was all the repetition of old-fashioned and disconnected exercises and high-sounding methods with a lot of uppity words that almost never meant anything to me. Singing didn't feel natural anymore, like it had when I was a boy on my own doing things my way. But, with a whole lot of singing and a whole lot of teaching others how to do it, I eventually got myself back to the joy and fun of singing.

I find it disheartening that so many people, young people especially, can't relax and just breathe, and easily let the sound come out. It's an amazing feeling that is not easy to articulate. But, when it's done right, it's almost like some sort of a high and to me it feels so freeing. Whatever sound I want to make I can do freely and easily. I mean, I can croon around a ballad and I can sing all up and down. It's just amazing how wonderful it feels when everything is working together.

I'm always wanting that for my students, too. That amazing feeling of ease and effortless fun of singing out loud. I say to them all the time, "Go out under a tree somewhere and relax, and just breathe. And while you're there maybe think about things a little bit differently. Think about what's happening at that moment. Breathe slowly and deeply. Let a song play in your head and softly follow the sound with your own voice. Don't think about it too much, just do it. Let your voice respond to your thoughts and your breathing. Ask yourself 'Am I having fun yet?' And feel the joyfulness of singing."

I tell 'em to "go sit underneath a tree," somewhere you can go and feel the power of your own voice. Find some place that you can watch and listen for the naturalness in your own singing. A place where you can pay attention to your body and how the breath moves it. Somewhere that you feel comfortable and at ease to sing out loud so you can make whatever sounds you can imagine. Some place peaceful and quiet with a minimum of distractions.

I know I must sound like some old hippie or new age guru talking about all this touchy, feely stuff – running around nekkid and sitting under trees. And while I will not confirm or deny whether I have run around the woods without my clothes. I can say, I've spent a lot of days sitting in the shade of trees doing a lot of thinking and even more experimenting. I also watched and listened to a lot of other singers -- good and bad, young and old, experienced and just beginning. That probably helped me the most to learn to listen, and hear what not to do as well as what to do.

And I had some good teachers, too-- three actually. And with all of them I asked a lot of questions. They taught me what they knew, and they taught me well. They were all willing to help me be the singer I was without trying to make me into what they thought a good singer ought to be.

I suppose that's why I started teaching. I wanted to do that for other singers, too. I didn't want all that learning to be lost. Still don't. And that's why I'm writing all about it here for you.

For me, singing better and being more creative has involved a whole lot of just fooling around, trying this and that to figure out for myself what was too much and what was not enough. To find the right balance of emotion, imagination, and actual singing. And remembering to have fun along the way.

Chapter Thirteen
DO YOU HAVE A QUESTION?

There are even now still a lot of singers and teachers who passionately believe in the conventional way of teaching, with all the standard exercises and peculiar "vocal methods," and antiquated ideas and rules. I know some of you have probably had one or two of those stereotypical lessons and never really understood what the heck you were being asked to do, but you gave it a try anyway. But unfortunately, while traditional teaching clearly works well for some singers, it doesn't work for all. Mostly, I think it doesn't work because good teaching and good learning means, meeting people where they are and not where they ought to be.

As you can probably tell by now, I'm not a very formal person. I don't go by titles or like to be called by my surname. I'm a pretty laid-back person with an organic teaching style that's mostly a conversation between two singers about whatever is happening at the time. I mostly use the "Socratic Method" of teaching, which simply means I ask a lot of questions and then, put most of the responsibility on you to come up with your own answers. And even if the answers are not always clear at first, I believe questions can still change things, just by the asking.

I teach by example. I teach the things I do. Things I think you should know. But that doesn't mean I expect you to have the same opinions or feelings or thoughts that I do. I believe everybody is uniquely different. I think I've been clear that I do not believe there is one right way to sing or swing a baseball bat, or one way to make a bed. But there are some out there who do. I can guarantee that there are a whole lot of people out there who will be more than happy to try to convince you that they know best about who can and cannot sing, or throw a ball, or dance, or do whatever. Everybody has an opinion.

Sure, there are performance standards for music and sports and dancing, and everything else under the sun. We all sort of know them and recognize them, particularly when we see or hear them. And with particular regard to singing, there is no question that some people do it better than others. But who gets to say what is good and what isn't? And what qualifies them to make that judgement? I believe that we each have to make those sorts of determinations for ourselves, based on our own measure of talent and our own ideas of what's good and what's not-so-good.

For instance, let's assume that as a professional musician and teacher I'm probably going to hear and judge a student's performance very differently than their loving parents who think everything they do is wonderful and brilliant. And that's okay. They are supposed to believe their kid is wonderful and brilliant because that's what they want to believe.

Truth is, we all hear what we want to hear and see what we want to see. That's how we all can look at the same thing and see something totally different. We hear and see things from our own biased perspective that's completely made up of our feelings, our thoughts, and our experiences.

I've had a whole mess of experiences, over the years, along with some pretty intense feelings, and even a deep thought or two every now and again. You've probably had plenty of your own, as well. That's what makes us who we are. That's what makes us do what we do, and, I think, what makes us want to get better at doing it -- whatever "it" is.

I always want to do better than I'm doing now. To know more and to do more. That's what I hope to inspire in you. And I hope that by sharing a little about my own experiences, you can understand more about where my way of thinking comes from and how and why it differs a bit from more conventional ways. And in turn, that might get you to think differently and start questioning some things, too.

I've never minded questions. And it makes me feel sort of powerful in a way when I have control of the question and the answer. I hope you will learn to enjoy answering questions by learning to ask them. I also hope you will develop a curious nature; and if you already have one, do your best to hold on to it. Keep in mind though, that not every question can be answered right away, or sometimes at all. And not every idea is a great idea. But what matters most is the thought that you put into the questions and answers and the time you spend considering each idea. It's about your process, not what happens at the end.

That's what all of this questioning is really all about. To encourage you to keep trying again and again; to follow your instincts and let the questions freely direct and redirect your thinking. And then, in time, you will come up with the best answers for you. You will figure out your own process for learning to sing better and being more creative.

That sort of sums up my whole philosophy, "You should rely on your own thoughts and judgments and trust yourself more than anyone else." This is what eventually leads you to your own technique. But, that doesn't mean you can't ask for help when you need it. I just think it's important to know why you're asking for help and what you expect that person to do that you can't do for yourself.

I never say to a student, "I think you should do this or do that." I just turn it back around and ask questions in hopes that I can get you to decide for yourself what you want to do and how you are going to go about it. But the answer isn't really important, it's what you do that counts. I believe if you want to get better at what you do, you've got to get out there and do it, all on your own.

For some of you, I understand that the idea of doing things on your own can be a little scary and maybe even a little risky, if you're not mindful. But whether you do it on your own or with outside help, there is still a lot of guess work and experimenting that has to happen. So, why not give it a try on your own? And when things don't go as planned, try to think more creatively and figure out a way to change things all together, and start again.

There are hundreds of teachers and even more books and articles on singing that discourage learning to sing on your own. Some, because of famous old traditions. And some, because of concerns for the potential for vocal damage. But the voice is a hardy and adaptable instrument and long term voice problems due to supposed vocal abuse are surprisingly rare.

Yes, we all know that vocal nodules are a common concern for young and inexperienced singers, but no more than with non-singers. You can just as easily develop vocal problems from yelling and screaming at a football game or talking across the table in a noisy bar, or even by coughing and clearing your throat a lot. The point is to be smart. Listen to your own voice. Trust your instincts.

It is true that I went to college and studied music and that I learned from others by watching and listening, but still I pretty much did things on my own. I questioned everything I was taught. I suppose I needed to decide for myself what I believed. And so, I kept at it until I knew it was right for me. I would go around trying out all kinds of sounds in all kinds of different ways and figured out what my voice was capable of doing and what it wasn't. I asked myself a million questions and tried to make sense of it all. And in time, I did. That's how come I believe you never know what you can do until you try.

It's a bit cliché, I know, but it's true. I see it all the time when I work with singers. When I look into their eyes and see them putting things together like a jigsaw puzzle. And when I hear subtle changes in their voices, so they sound more like themselves. I watch them start to loosen up and have fun. And my part in it all is just to be a guide, directing them but not doing it for them.

Anything you want to learn, pretty much, you can teach yourself. You just have to want to create something unique and extraordinary and learn to rely on your own judgement. Trust yourself. Be confident. Take risks to do something that you've never done. And be willing to succeed and fail at the same time.

I mean, if you really want to sing and be more creative, I say, "Go for it," and have fun while you're doing it. Life is too short to not do what you want to do. As far as I'm concerned, everybody can sing and everybody is creative to some degree. I just don't think that everybody has enough confidence in themselves to put it all out there. Like stripping down and running nekkid in the woods.

But with learning comes confidence. And the more you know, the more confident you feel. The more confident you feel, the more comfortable you become with yourself. And I think that's a good place to start.

It was such an eye-opener for me when I first started to see how this all affects frightened and young college-aged musicians, insecure and unsure about what they are doing. I wanted to help them find their confidence; to encourage and teach them to do their own thing. To hold on to the distinctively unique qualities of their own voice. And to be free to choose and do things in their own way and not just do the same old thing the same old way as everybody else.

At some point, I started to pay more attention to what was going on in their heads and their hearts, and not worry so much about the rest. I got away from the overly-technical talk and avoided vocal exercises. I encouraged them to think differently and do differently. And to not get too caught up in **how** to sing, but to **just sing**.

Chapter Fourteen
WHAT ARE YOU GOING TO DO NOW?

Well, I think I'll let you go now so that you can get started figuring all this stuff out for yourself. I feel like it's okay to leave you now, with your own questions and thoughts and ideas. I will, however, put one last question to you. "What are you going to do now?"

And not for nothing, you came all this way with me, so I hope you will at least try my ideas and see if they work for you. 'Cause if you do, I think you'll be singing better and creating more than maybe you ever thought possible. It worked for me and a lot of other singers I've taught over the years.

When I was a kid it was joyous to sing. That's all I ever thought about. Not as a career, but rather just for the sheer fun of it. I never complained about being bored like some kids complain today. I had fun back then, but looking back, it was just me enjoying figuring things out for myself. Learning all the stuff I still think about every day. You'd be surprised at how much of what I learned when I was younger I still make use of today.

But, once you figure it all out it stays with you. That's your technique. It's your way of doing things. And it's always there when you need it. So, why not give it a try and see whether it works? You will figure out your way and other people will have theirs. No two of us are the same, so don't be afraid to take risks and make mistakes because you will learn from them and be better for it.

Learn to breathe slowly and naturally because your body needs air. Learn to listen and try to hear the sound you want to make in your head before you ever open your mouth. And when you open it to sing, try to relax and feel the air move through the space. And then, try not to interfere with whatever happens to it or whatever it does. Let the sound go and just focus on creating the sound that you imagined. Sounds easy, right?

Well, to me it's easy. For me, singing is easy and teaching someone else to do it is easy, too. But that's because I already know how to do it. I've been singing for over fifty years, now. I've already done all the experiments and asked all the questions, made all the silly faces and goofy noises. And, I've worked with hundreds of singers over the years, and believe me, I've seen and heard it all.

Still, I understand that if you don't know how to sing already, or want to sing better than you do now, maybe for you it might not feel so easy to do. But hopefully you feel at least a little freer now to experiment and find what's completely right for you. I mean, the pressure's off. You have the okay to do things differently. To think new thoughts in new ways. To try again and again until it feels right, or if not right at least better. You just have to be willing to try.

Don't let fear stop you from trying. If you want to sing but aren't sure if you can, do it anyway. Even if it doesn't work out at first, you can always try something different the next time. Just get out there and do the best you can.

You can start by finding a song you like. A song that you know both the melody and lyrics. Sing it when you are in the shower and when you are in the car. Sing it while you fold the laundry and as you sweep the floor or vacuum the rug. Ask yourself what does it feel like when you are singing the song? Then think creatively about your answer. And if someone else doesn't agree with what you are doing or the way you do it, that's their problem, not yours.

That reminds me of a quote, "What other people think about me is none of my business." I don't know who said it first, but it was my wonderfully wise mother-in-law who said it to me. But the point is, don't worry about things you can't control, but rather focus on changing all the things you can. And while you may not be able to sing like Luciano Pavarotti or Aretha Franklin, it is possible to work with what you've got to become the best singer you can be.

And don't get caught up comparing yourself to other singers. There's no point to it. Of course, you are going to be better than some and some are going to be better than you. But who gets to say? Because everyone has their own opinions and different ideas about what's good and bad. For instance, one man's Luther Vandross might be another man's William Hung, (although, I can't imagine it).

But who could have imagined early on that Madonna would become a musical icon of the 80s, or Britney Spears in the 90s. Neither one are what I would call, "a natural singer." But both are still making records and playing concerts today. Thanks mostly to pitch correction technology, like Auto-Tune and audiences' willingness to turn a blind eye to lip syncing live and singing to backing tracks. But who's to say what's good and what's not. And it doesn't matter whether you agree or disagree, only that you understand it is all relative. It is simply a matter of likes and dislikes.

So, what's to stop you from getting out there and giving it a try yourself. Whether you do it the same old way as everybody else or do it on your own. What's more important is for you to be honest, but fair to your own self and give yourself the same consideration that you would give to any other person. And to expect as much encouragement and understanding for yourself as you would expect from any other singer and teacher.

But before you decide whether to teach yourself or go outside for help, I hope you will take time to stand back, or maybe even find a tree and sit down in the shade, and look at yourself from a distance. Don't judge. Just watch and listen. And don't worry about what others think as much as what you think. And hopefully, you'll become your own best teacher.

Made in the USA
Lexington, KY
10 July 2017